7/12

D1116330

MILITARY MACHINES

# MILITARY SHIPS

by Barbara Alpert

**Consulting Editor:** Gail Saunders-Smith, PhD

**Consultant:** Raymond L. Puffer, PhD
Historian, Ret.
Edwards Air Force Base History Office

CAPSTONE PRESS
a capstone imprint

Pebble Plus is published by Capstone Press,
1710 Roe Crest Drive, North Mankato, Minnesota 56003.
www.capstonepub.com

Copyright © 2012 by Capstone Press, a Capstone imprint. All rights reserved.
No part of this publication may be reproduced in whole or in part, or stored in a retrieval system, or transmitted in any
form or by any means, electronic, mechanical, photocopying, recording, or otherwise, without written permission of the
publisher. For information regarding permission, write to Capstone Press,
1710 Roe Crest Drive, North Mankato, Minnesota 56003.

Books published by Capstone Press are manufactured with paper
containing at least 10 percent post-consumer waste.

*Library of Congress Cataloging-in-Publication Data*
Alpert, Barbara.
  Military ships / by Barbara Alpert.
       p. cm.—(Pebble plus. Military machines)
  Includes bibliographical references and index.
  Summary: "Simple text and full-color photographs describe various military ships"—Provided by publisher.
    ISBN 978-1-4296-7572-7 (library binding)
    ISBN 978-1-4296-7885-8 (paperback)
  1.  Warships—United States—Juvenile literature.  I. Title.
  VA55.A75 2012
  623.8250973—dc23                                              2011021658

**Editorial Credits**
Erika L. Shores, editor; Kyle Grenz, designer; Kathy McColley, production specialist

**Photo Credits**
U.S. Coast Guard Photo by PO2 Prentice Danner, 11
U.S. Navy photo by General Dynamics Electric Boat, 17, MC2 Gary A. Prill, 15, MC2 Gary A. Prill, cover, MC2 Rafael
        Figueroa Medina, 21, MC3 Nicholas Hall, 13, MC3 Patrick Heil, 9, MC3 Shawn J. Stewart, 7, MCSN Jared M.
        King, 5, PH1 Richard J. Brunson, 19

**Artistic Effects**
Shutterstock: Hitdelight

## Note to Parents and Teachers

The Military Machines series supports national science standards related to science, technology,
and society. This book describes and illustrates military ships. The images support early readers
in understanding the text. The repetition of words and phrases helps early readers learn new
words. This book also introduces early readers to subject-specific vocabulary words, which are
defined in the Glossary section. Early readers may need assistance to read some words and to
use the Table of Contents, Glossary, Read More, Internet Sites, and Index sections of the book.

Printed in the United States of America in North Mankato, Minnesota.
052012    006719R

# Table of Contents

# What Are Military Ships?

Military ships sail all over the world. Wherever there is deep water, the U.S. Armed Forces has ships ready for battle.

# Parts of Military Ships

A captain commands a ship from the bridge. Looking out through big windows, the captain tells the crew where to steer the ship.

Military ship floors are
called decks.
Fighter jets land on
aircraft carrier flight decks.

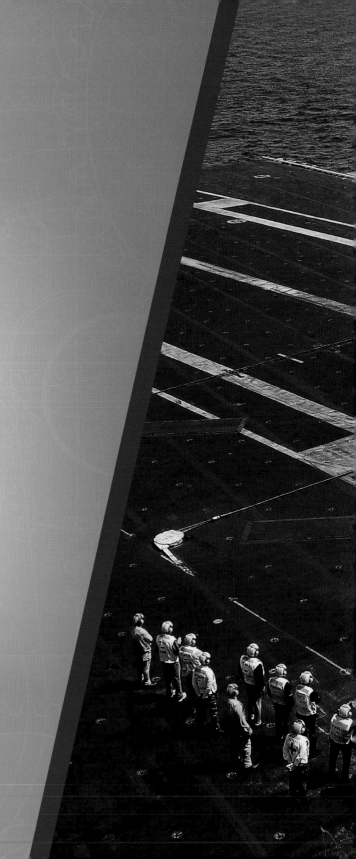

Ships called icebreakers have extra-strong hulls. Icebreakers cut through frozen oceans without their hulls cracking.

# Ships in the Military

Aircraft carriers are the largest military ships. More than 60 planes fit on the flight deck. It's longer than three football fields.

Destroyers protect other ships

from enemy attacks.

Destroyers use sonar equipment

to find enemy submarines.

Submarines travel on top of and under the water. They dive 800 feet (244 meters) below the surface. Submarines shoot missiles at enemy targets.

Amphibious dock landing ships carry amphibious vehicles. These vehicles float on water and travel onto shore to deliver troops and supplies.

# Military Machines

Military ships may travel alone or with many other ships. These mighty military machines are always on the go.

# Glossary

**amphibious**—able to operate on water and on land

**Armed Forces**—the whole military; the U.S. Armed Forces include the Army, Navy, Air Force, Marine Corps, and Coast Guard

**bridge**—the command center of a ship

**deck**—a wood or metal floor on a ship or boat that runs from one end to the other

**dive**—to steer toward the ocean floor

**hull**—the outer part of a ship

**icebreaker**—a ship that can cut through frozen oceans without damage to itself

**missile**—a weapon that is fired at or dropped on a target

**sonar**—a system of sending sound waves to find objects in the water by listening for an echo

# Read More

**Jackson, Kay.** *Navy Ships in Action.* Amazing Military Vehicles. New York: PowerKids Press, 2009.

**Tagliaferro, Linda.** *Who Lands Planes on a Ship?: Working on an Aircraft Carrie*r. Wild Work. Chicago: Raintree, 2011.

**Zuehlke, Jeffrey.** *Warships.* Pull Ahead Books. Minneapolis.: Lerner Publications Co., 2006.

# Internet Sites

FactHound offers a safe, fun way to find Internet sites related to this book. All of the sites on FactHound have been researched by our staff.

Here's all you do:

Visit *www.facthound.com*

Type in this code: 9781429675727

 Super-cool stuff! Check out projects, games and lots more at www.capstonekids.com

# Index

Word Count: 174

Grade: 1

Early-Intervention Level: 21